Abby Can...Play!

ISBN 979-8-89130-781-0 (paperback)
ISBN 979-8-89130-782-7 (digital)

Christian Faith Publishing
832 Park Avenue
Meadville, PA 16335
www.christianfaithpublishing.com

Illustrated by: Jeeva

Printed in the United States of America

Abby Can...Play!

A story about inclusion

Lisa Molina

Abby is a little girl who was born with Down syndrome. This means that her brain learns and understands things in a way that is different from most children her age. It also means she looks and speaks just a little different from most other children.

Sometimes her friends will ask, "What's wrong with her?"

Sometimes her classmates will ask, "Why can't she speak clearly, read, or understand math like us?"

But there is so much Abby *can* do! Nothing is "wrong" with her. She was born to be exactly who she is—just like you were born to be exactly who you are!

Abby can play! She loves to play with friends on the playground at school or at the park.

Abby can swing! It's one of her favorite things to do! She also loves going down slides!

She can run and prance! Abby loves a good game of tag. Sometimes she prances like a horse when she moves!

She can throw a Frisbee and catch a ball!

4

Abby loves playing with bubbles—blowing them and popping them is so much fun!

She can bounce! Abby loves to use the trampoline in her backyard as well as bounce houses at birthday parties!

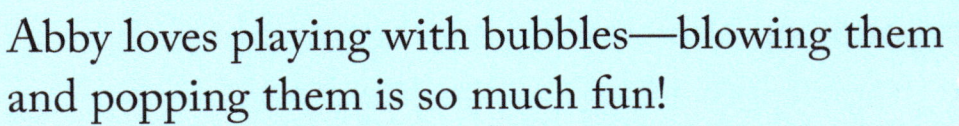

Abby can imagine! Even when Abby doesn't have friends around to play with, she imagines that she does!

Abby can play dress-up! Dressing up as a princess is one of her favorite things to do!

Abby also loves to play with dolls. She can arrange her doll furniture in the dollhouse and have her dolls talk to one another as they play together!

Abby loves to perform! Sometimes she enjoys acting out stories or movies as though she is on a stage!

She can sing! It is often easier for Abby to sing words clearly than to speak them. And she loves using a microphone!

Abby can dance! Listening to music is another one of her favorite things to do. And sometimes the music moves her to dance and spin around!

8

She can learn! Abby practices writing her letters and numbers at school. She has also started learning how to read!

She can memorize! Abby remembers the words to songs she learned several years ago!

Abby can make her own bed! She can brush
her teeth, choose the clothes she wants to wear,
and brush her hair.

11

She can show kindness to animals! Abby loves to pet her dog friends!

Abby can wonder! She often wants to know what her family and friends are doing. She wonders when she can spend more time with them.

13

She can pray! Abby loves to pray for all her family members and friends.

She can hug! Abby cares about others. She shows love and concern for her family and friends by giving them lots of hugs!

15

Abby can bake! She really enjoys helping her mom and older brother make cookies, cakes, and pies.

16

She can cook other things too! Scrambled
eggs is one of Abby's favorite foods to cook
for breakfast.

She can laugh! There are things that Abby
finds funny—like playing tricks on her brother.
So, yes, sometimes she can also annoy others!

Abby is curious! She loves to discover how things work. She is trying to learn how to play the piano and the guitar!

Abby can help in the garden! She loves to water the plants and trees. She also enjoys digging in the dirt and harvesting fruits and vegetables!

Abby is full of energy and loves to keep busy! She is a happy child most of the time, but she also has other feelings too. Just like everyone else, she can sometimes feel sad, mad, or frustrated.

So, really, Abby can do many of the things that most kids can do. She's actually a lot more like you than she is different! And that's exactly how she was meant to be!

To Parents, Teachers, and Caregivers

It is so important to talk about all the ways children with disabilities are similar to typically developing children.

It's important to encourage questions about children who have disabilities while in a safe and judgement-free environment. Please remind your children or students that no one is exactly like everyone else—even identical twins have differences that make them unique from each other.

If children notice differences and seem reluctant to interact with someone who has a disability, please remind them that everyone enjoys a smile and a friendly hello or wave.

If you aren't sure how a child with a disability may react to engagement from your child, please check first with the parent or caregiver who is with the child.

Thank you for remembering that we are all unique in our own ways. We all want to have friends. We all express feelings in different ways. We all need to feel cared for and loved!

Lisa Molina
Mother of Abby

About the Author

Lisa Molina is an elementary school teacher of twenty-four years who recently transitioned into homeschool teaching for her twelve-year-old daughter, Abby, who was born with Down syndrome. Lisa also has a seventeen-year-old son who is getting ready to graduate from high school. She has been happily married to her amazing husband for twenty-one years.

Throughout Lisa's years in the classroom and her time raising Abby, she has been continuously learning about the various ways all children learn and adapt as they grow. Most children who have special needs are not significantly different from typically developing children in that regard. This book is meant to serve as a way to connect the commonalities among both types of children rather than focus solely on the differences.

Printed in the USA
CPSIA information can be obtained
at www.ICGtesting.com
CBHW040115301024
16598CB00028B/1075